MW00698326

BROOKE MITCHELL

FRIENDS IN HIM

OUR WALK OF FAITH

A Three-Part Parable of Divine Love

CREATION
HOUSE

Friends in Him by Brooke Mitchell
Published by Creation House
A Charisma Media Company
600 Rinehart Road
Lake Mary, Florida 32746
www.charismamedia.com

Unless otherwise noted, all Scripture quotations are from the New
American Standard Bible–Updated Edition, Copyright © 1960, 1962,
1963, 1968, 1971, 1972, 1973, 1975, 1977, 1995 by The Lockman
Foundation. Used by permission. (www.Lockman.org)

Scripture quotations marked nlt are from the Holy Bible, New Living
Translation, copyright © 2007. Used by permission of Tyndale House
Publishers, Inc., Wheaton, IL 60189. All rights reserved.

Design Director: Bill Johnson
Cover design by Nathan Morgan

Visit the author's website: www.ThroneRoomConsulting.com.

Library of Congress Cataloging-in-Publication Data: 2013952179
International Standard Book Number: 978-1-62136-699-7
E-book International Standard Book Number: 978-1-62136-700-0

While the author has made every effort to provide accurate
telephone numbers and Internet addresses at the time of publication,
neither the publisher nor the author assumes any responsibility for
errors or for changes that occur after publication.

First edition

14 15 16 17 18 — 9 8 7 6 5 4 3 2 1
Printed in Canada

This book is dedicated to the Father, Son, and Holy Spirit and their continued authorship in each of our love stories.

Fixing our eyes on Jesus, the author and perfecter of faith...

—HEBREWS 12:2

CONTENTS

PREFACE

EAR FRIEND IN Him,
Through divine sovereignty you have picked up a three-part parable called *Friends in Him: Our Walk of Faith.* This resource is written for women with the specific intent of ministering through a real-life love story between a twenty-first century woman and the Lord. Inspiration for this project resulted from a literal daily walk of faith and an eyewitness account of "friends in Him." It is our prayer that this resource will encourage and inspire you in your walk of faith, as well as guide you to the specific calling and plan God has for your life.

This book is tiny in stature but packs a lot of punch in power, purpose, prophetic insight, and application. As you read the three different parts you will notice the same pattern throughout the text. You will read an excerpt of testimony written in parable form followed by a "step." The parable is written so you can identify with the characters and situations facing women today. The step is a call to action in your personal faith-walk with the Lord. The steps are not rigid, ritualistic rules but rather identified for insight and understanding as you begin writing your own love story with the Lord through the Holy Spirit.

An interwoven theme throughout the entire book is the gospel message presented through present-day, relevant application. The testimony excerpts are evangelistic in their prose. The goal is for the testimonies shared to teach you about God's revelation through faith and obedience. The steps are written with a discipleship framework in mind. The goal is for these sections to inspire actions that in turn reach you and result in you reaching others through your personal calling.

It is, however, recommended that you read each of the parable texts in sequential order. This first part is the foundational text of testimony and also application in which the Lord builds and advances the stories and steps following in the second and third sections. The second part builds on both the testimony and progression of steps that occur in the walk of faith. The testimony and application will prayerfully equip you to persevere through the "newlywed" days of your calling. The third part of the book presents testimony and application that will empower you through your love-relationship with the Lord.

The people, places, and stories shared are all real, yet no names are mentioned throughout the story. This is intentional and models the same discernment Jesus used when speaking to the crowds in parables. He never called out an individual as an example; rather, He attributed the person or meaning to a characteristic. This helped the audience focus on the teaching and meaning rather than the individual person.

Just as the Father, Son, and Holy Spirit have separate roles yet are One in purpose, *Friends in Him* presents three separate parts but One message. There are three parts but one book with the prayer for each testimony to teach and each step to reach in application to the love-story God wants to individually author for each of us.

Then those who feared the Lord spoke to one another, and the Lord gave attention and heard it, and a book of remembrance was written before Him for those who fear the Lord and who esteem His name.

—MALACHI 3:16

PART I:

THEY LIVED HAPPILY EVER AFTER

You have taken account of my wanderings; Put my tears in Your bottle. Are *they* not in Your book?

—PSALM 56:8

Friday, August 30, 2002

Call to Me and I will answer you, and I will tell you great and mighty things, which you do not know.

—Jeremiah 33:3

It was the end of the only life She had ever Known. Within a single second at 1:30 in the afternoon and a signature scribbled on the dotted line, She was alone. "God, if you don't do something, we won't make it. I have two Children to raise. I am sick. I can't work. I need help," She cried aloud as the finale of an adulterous twenty-four-year marriage to her First Love came to an abrupt end.

Of course, the story did not begin how it ended. And from the outside She appeared to be living the fairy-tale life. She lived in a gated community, drove luxury cars, dressed in designer clothing, taught in a prestigious school, and owned a prosperous business. Her family excelled in their pursuits. However, the pressure to produce the perfect family, in the middle of a decaying marriage, had positioned her flat on her back in bed with a chronic illness.

She returned home to an empty house, which felt

familiar. But She was consumed with a different kind of aloneness this time. Her body ached with the fatigue and finality of the day's events.

However, the answering machine's blinking light signaling a message provided a beacon of light in her spirit. *I wonder who called me?*, She silently questioned. As She listened to the recorded message She did not recognize the voice of the caller, but oddly the man on the other end knew all about her!

Her spirit stirred and curiosity piqued. The caller requested to meet with her. There was a limited time the invitation was extended due to a busy travel schedule. The call was purely professional and an offer to thank her for faithfully supporting the Organization. Suddenly, fear and hesitation gripped her. *This is a scam and can't be real. Single women shouldn't respond to strangers in today's world.* She then noticed the message was left at 1:30. This was the exact time She was signing her name to the end of the only life She had Known and was crying aloud to God.

As She milled around the house folding laundry She could not shake the irony of the timing of the caller's message and request. She spoke with her friend over the day's events and her friend, a Counselor, advised it was too risky to meet with a stranger, confirming her fear. She counseled and warned that it was not proper for her to be alone with this man.

Even though She was hesitant and unsure She acted and responded to the caller's request to return the call. As general introductions were made, She knew there was credibility and authenticity in the sound of his voice. She invited the Divine Appointment into her home to speak and meet with both her and her Children the following day. As the day came to an end, She went to bed with a sense of anticipation and expectation of what tomorrow would hold.

STEP 1: CONVERSATION

> Even though She was hesitant and doubtful She
> acted and responded to the call and request.

There are moments in our lives that decidedly separate our experienced past from our not-yet-experienced future. When we encounter situations or circumstances that are outside our ability to change or control, God is the only One with the power, purpose, and plan. We must always call out to God, not as a last resort, but as the starting place. In our walk with God, speaking to Him is the first step.

As our story begins, She is faced with many choices that appear to be insignificant, yet are paramount in determining the outcome of her Happily Ever After. However, the entire story begins when She literally calls aloud to God. Whenever we initiate a conversation with God, He will always respond. When we talk to God, He begins orchestrating events and circumstances to answer our prayers. At the time His responses may not be immediately recognized, but we must be willing to speak to God, because He is the only one with the plan and purpose for our present circumstance and future calling. And God is never late. At the exact second it may have appeared too late for God to intervene. However, when She called to God, He began to orchestrate events in the natural for a Divine Appointment that would forever shift the entire direction of her life.

It is also important to realize that when we first begin to speak to God it will take action on our part to respond to an unfamiliar voice that is at first Unknown. This is very similar to the voice of the Divine Appointment She heard on the answering machine message. Just like relationships with new friends, there is a moment of introduction and becoming acquainted with the sound, tone, and sincerity of one's voice. After we speak to God He will always speak back to us (more on this in following steps). At the same time this occurs, there is another voice that will begin to speak. The voice of natural human reasoning can be an enemy to our ability to respond to God's activity.

When we begin speaking to God in the natural there is a shift of divine activity on our behalf in the spiritual. At the same time, there will be opposition in both the natural and spiritual against us to take action to respond to God's activity. The opposition to God's plan and purposes being achieved always begins and ends with Satan. Fear, doubt, and unbelief were tactics of Satan to prevent an opportunity that would redefine the future for not only her but countless other souls and lives. Once we take the step to speak to God, we must continue to move forward in listening to and obeying His voice in order to change our lives.

Are you willing to call out to God? God only requires us to take one step at a time. The first step is calling to God. Then pay attention to the shift in circumstances and situations as they align themselves in answer to your prayer. He is waiting to answer and act on your behalf. Whatever circumstance, situation, or concern that is pressing to you, He wants you to talk to Him about it.

> Call to Me and I will answer you, and I will tell you great and mighty things, which you do not know.
> —JEREMIAH 33:3

SATURDAY, AUGUST 31, 2002

And Jesus said…"Today salvation has come to this house."

—LUKE 19:9

THE DOORBELL FINALLY rang mid-afternoon. All day She had an internal battle over whether or not to invite the Divine Appointment into her home. Her mind was bombarded with thoughts such as, *You are putting your Children at risk to invite this man into your home. You know nothing about him. He's only visiting with you because the Organization needs money. They care nothing about you.* All day She considered graciously bowing out of the meeting; however, She could not shake the timing of the call to the very moment of her prayer to God.

The chime of the doorbell sealed the finality of the meeting. *It's time. He's here.* She silently braced herself for an evening of small talk. And with the opening of her front door, She invited the Divine Appointment to enter her home, to meet her Children and to speak with her about the Organization.

Once the Divine Appointment sat down at the kitchen

table and the conversation unfolded, it was clearly Known the character and virtue of the Organization's representative. She was refreshed by the kindness extended to her and her Children. She was encouraged by the joy, energy, and excitement over serving God on behalf of the Organization. She was relieved by the sincere love shared for his wife and children. And She also realized that every fear, hesitation, or warning received from others was not true, as it was clearly Known that the evening was based on the common support for the Organization. She was touched that God answered her prayer in such a way to extend the refreshment of being in the presence of a man without hidden motives or an agenda that would harm her family. In her deepest moment of fear and abandonment, God sent in the Unknown, through the Divine Appointment, to make His presence Known.

She noticed that several times it was made Known that She should read the *Resource* by the Author. Each time She acknowledged that the resource sounded fascinating, and She looked forward to having a new book to read. Yet the persistence and urgency of this request kept increasing, and it was finally Known that the Organization wanted to purchase a copy of the book for her—that evening! It was certainly a surprise, and the uncertainty of the Unknown crept back into mind. *It was not proper for her to be alone with this man*, the Counselor's words replayed silently. However, She responded, "I would love to receive this gift."

The drive to and from the bookstore was filled with conversation and laughter. The evening ended with continued thanks and praise for the work of the Organization. As the events of the day came to an end, She went to bed for the second night in a row with anticipation and expectation of what the days ahead would hold for her and her family. She had a new book to read and was touched that the Organization made it Known how important She was to the continued success of its work. She was also relieved that She and her Children had done nothing improper. Maybe She was not as alone as She thought; it seemed like there was hope remaining in the future. She wanted to learn more.

STEP 2: CONFESSION

She responded, "I would love to receive this gift."

God's love story for mankind began in the Garden of Eden after God rebuked Satan for deceiving Adam and Eve with the Unknown fruit of the tree of knowledge.

> He shall bruise you on the head, and you shall bruise him on the heel.
>
> —GENESIS 3:15

The first prophecy of the power, redemption, and pursuit Jesus would bring to Satan's attempt to entice mankind with the Unknown was clearly made Known by God in the beginning. The same pattern exists for women today. The platform may have changed since the Garden of Eden, but the plan of salvation over what the enemy posits as Unknown—to women in particular—has not changed.

In our moments of being alone, we as women are vulnerable to the uncertainty of the Unknown. Eve was alone in the Garden of Eden when Satan approached her. We must recognize that God's plan for salvation supersedes and precedes the natural order of our circumstances, feeling, or perception. When alone with her thoughts, fear, hesitation, and doubt crept in, convincing her that the activity She was discerning from God might in fact not be true. This is the same tactic Satan used against Eve to convince and confuse her against the voice and activity of God. In the twenty-first century there are many more concerns and realities that we face in our world than Eve faced in the garden; however, the ambush and false authority of the enemy has not changed.

God has a plan for both earthly and eternal salvation for each of our lives. Jesus saved us from our sins once and for all on Calvary. In addition, there is earthly salvation known as deliverance, where God intervenes to rescue us from past or present circumstances contrary to His future plan for our lives. To receive both eternal and earthly salvation requires believing through faith in God's promises.

> For by grace you have been saved through faith; and that not of yourselves, *it is* the gift of God.
> —EPHESIANS 2:8

Just as She accepted the gift of the *Resource* despite hesitation and uncertainty, we too must be willing to step forward in faith to believe and receive God's plan of salvation for our eternal destiny and earthly experience. At that time She agreed to receive the gift, She had no idea how God would use that resource to transform the entire future direction of her life and calling. When we accept the gift of salvation God offers, we too are aligning our lives in agreement to be used and transformed by God.

In our walk with God we must be willing to take steps of faith. Foundational to our walk of faith are believing and receiving God's plan of salvation for our lives given through Jesus Christ, God's Son. If you "confess with your mouth Jesus *as* Lord, and believe in your heart that God raised Him from the dead, you will be saved" (Rom. 10:9). Also, we must not settle for waiting to receive this eternal salvation in heaven. By knowing what God says and believing in His promises, we have access to earthly salvation during our lives. The Author's *Resource* is recommended to understand who, what, when, where, and how God speaks directly and personally to each believer. Once we receive our salvation, we become a part of God's Organization, known as the church, a body of believers throughout the ends of the earth.

Have you received the free gift of salvation? God only requires us to take one step at a time. He offers forgiveness for our sins and deliverance from our situations. Do not be deceived or confused by the Unknown, but recognize and receive that God wants to make His presence Known to you. While there is much more to learn and understand in our walk of faith with God, believing in His promise of salvation is the foundational faith step.

> Today salvation has come to this house.
>
> —LUKE 19:9

Saturday, September 21, 2002

But Jesus turning and seeing her said, "Daughter, take courage; your faith has made you well." At once the woman was made well.

—Matthew 9:22

SHE CONTINUED TO stay busy. Well, as busy and active as possible, considering She was in her third year of battling Chronic Fatigue. Typically, a day consisted of asking herself if She had enough energy to brush her teeth or blow dry her hair. However, She had recently been mixing some new activities into her daily options. For example, She had absorbed the *Resource,* having read and then reread it several times. It was amazing to learn that God wanted a personal relationship with her. She also learned that the Holy Spirit has a personality and speaks whatever He hears the Father say.

Being raised in the South and having attended Church most of her life, learning about the Holy Spirit was something new. She had visited her friend's (the Counselor's) church on a couple of occasions. This was a place where the

Holy Spirit was welcome in worship, through the preaching, and at the altar. Although She attended Church, She had never seen or experienced anything like this atmosphere! At the end of the sermon the Prophet called for people to come to the altar to pray. He wanted to lay hands on and pray for healing over the sick.

Thankfully, the Counselor sat on the front row, so She did not have far to walk. With one more step She was at the altar being prayed over in a new language. She told the Lord in her heart, *You are the same yesterday, today, and forever. You healed when you walked on this earth. Thank you for the day when You heal me.* The prayer ended, so She and Chronic Fatigue walked back to the pew. She left the building still very weak.

That service had been weeks ago. She did not doubt God could and would heal her, as She continued to lay flat on her back on the couch. This particular Saturday night She kept sensing a strong urge that God wanted her to pray. She continued to dismiss the promptings and reasoned, *I will, God. Let me finish these dishes, and then I will pray.* An overwhelming flood of urgency came into her spirit, and She remembered the importance of learning about immediate obedience from the *Resource.* She rose from the couch, dismissed the dishes waiting to be washed, and walked into her bedroom.

As she prayed, another prompting to open her Bible came to mind. Not knowing many verses or even where to look, She literally flipped opened her Bible. She looked at the page and suddenly her eyes read Matthew 9:22: "But Jesus turning and seeing her said, 'Daughter, take courage; your faith has made you well.' At once the woman was made well." Instantly, she believed and received God's written Word over her health and healing. Chronic Fatigue was immediately removed from her body. The Doctor had told her there was no cure for her illness, but She knew that God could and would heal her on His timetable. Like the refrain of the familiar tune, She would never fail to remember the twenty-first of September.

STEP 3: COURAGE

> She did not doubt God could and would heal her, as
> She continued to lay flat on her back on the couch.

We have access, through Jesus, to be healed of any sickness or disease in our physical bodies: "by His scourging we are healed" (Isa. 53:5). God does not show favoritism in who He decides to heal from sickness and disease. Healing is a right, not a privilege in the kingdom of God.

> Your kingdom come. Your will be done, On earth as
> it is in heaven.
>
> —MATTHEW 6:10

Once we receive our salvation through Jesus Christ, we are dual citizens of a heavenly and earthly kingdom.

Is there sickness, suffering, or disease in heaven? No. Is their sickness, suffering, or disease on earth? Yes. Is it God's will for His children in heaven for there to be sickness and disease? No, "And no resident will say, 'I am sick'" (Isa. 33:24). Therefore, it is not God's will for His children on earth to coexist with sickness and disease. We must not only believe but receive through the name of Jesus, the blood of Jesus, and the Word of Jesus our healing on earth as it is in heaven.

God's plan for healing is not limited to a particular church culture. God's healing is activated through faith, executed through the written Word of God, and received by faith. In other words, the Prophet who She prayed with demonstrated his faith that God could and would heal. The timing with which She received her healing from Chronic Fatigue was not immediate (although God can and will instantly provide healing). However, once the Word was released on Saturday, September 21, 2002, under the guidance of the Holy Spirit, supernatural healing was released. Again, She had to have faith to not only believe the written Word but to also receive her healing.

God uses people, such as the Prophet and friend (the Counselor), to execute His plan for our lives, but His primary tool is always His Word. The written Word of God is equivalent to victory in every area of our life: God's Word equals Victory. Once the Word speaks there is no reversing or changing the circumstance or situation; however, God moves and responds to our faith. Just as She never doubted there would be a moment of healing, we too must not doubt or enter into unbelief against the promises in God's Word.

It requires another step and willingness on our part to move forward with faith; we cannot retreat backward and receive the Victory simultaneously. For example, She had to step forward from her front row seat to demonstrate faith and enter into agreement with the Prophet when receiving a prayer for healing. In addition, God will often call us away from our comfort zone and into new cultures or environments to advance the next step of His plan over us.

Do you need healing? God only requires us to take one step at a time. Jesus wants you to know Him not only as Savior but also as Healer. Believe and receive the written Word of God over your infirmity. The Holy Spirit is a gentleman. He will meet you right where you are and escort you into Jesus' presence through the Father's written Word.

> But Jesus turning and seeing her said, "Daughter, take courage; your faith has made you well." At once the woman was made well.
>
> —Matthew 9:22

WEDNESDAY, JULY 30, 2003

"For I will restore you to health And I will heal you of your wounds," declares the Lord, "Because they have called you an outcast, saying, '...no one cares for her.'"

—JEREMIAH 30:17

THE MONTHS FOLLOWING her healing were productive (to say the least). Having lain flat on her back for over three years and after receiving a divine healing, She was back in the game called Life. Her house had never been cleaner, and She even found fulfillment in the ability to complete multiple errands in the same day! For the first time in over twenty-four years She was independent. Her divorce was finalized in January 2003. She was healthy, and She sensed God's activity in her daily life. She was enjoying reconnecting with past friends, as well as connecting with new friends in the Single Ministry at her Church.

In fact, one of the men in the Singles Ministry asked her out on several occasions to dinner and the movies. The Companion provided conversation, comfort, and counsel during the months of their courtship. Oddly, She awoke on Tuesday, July 29, 2003, with thoughts that her Companion was under spiritual warfare. Later that same day, She spoke with her Companion only to learn that the courtship must end due to confusion and uncertainty. Having already made dinner plans, She met with her Companion that same evening, and they parted ways on peaceful and respectful terms.

As she awoke to the reality of another day classified as *alone*, She reflected on her desire for love. She hoped one day to have a relationship where love was given and received freely without fear of betrayal or rejection. Her entire life her heart's cry had been to be a wife to a man that loved and cherished her as much as She respected and valued him. Following a divorce, responding to the Companion and having this relationship too come to an abrupt end, She was deeply crushed again by the rawness of the breakup and the wound to her heart.

As She began the following morning with a daily quiet time and Bible study, She was drawn in by the Teacher's devotional lesson, which was on the person of the Holy Spirit. She was intrigued that the Teacher shared the Holy Spirit's desire to have a personal love-relationship with each believer. He affirmed that the Holy Spirit has a personality; speaks; and promises to never leave, fail, or forsake us. This was exactly the love-relationship She was interested in pursuing. At that moment, She was introduced to the Holy Spirit, and her love-relationship with the Lord began. He has never broken up or broken off their relationship, and neither has She.

STEP 4: COMFORT

> She hoped one day to have a relationship where love was given and received freely without fear of betrayal or rejection.

Just as we all have different roles and duties in our relationships and jobs, the same is true of God the Father, God the Son, and God the Holy Spirit. Within our family units we may be called daughters, granddaughters, sisters, aunts, nieces, mothers, grandmothers, wives, widows. Within our jobs some of us may be called teacher, maid, sales clerk, shop owner, receptionist, student, housewife, or nurse. We are the same person with different names that correspond to our duty, obligation, role, or assignment within the various spheres of our influence. The same is true of the Father, Son, and Holy Spirit. The Holy Spirit's job is to speak what He hears the Father speak. The Holy Spirit's assignment on this earth is to point people to Jesus. He will never draw attention to Himself but desires us to be transformed into the likeness of Christ through His indwelling power.

The moment the gift of salvation through Jesus is received, each believer also receives the indwelling presence and power of the Holy Spirit. Following Jesus' earthly ministry and His death, burial, and resurrection, He ascended back into heaven. We are part of the twenty-first century church and body of believers and realize that Jesus is not physically walking and talking on the earth in our generation. Before Jesus ascended into heaven He said, "But I tell you the truth, it is to your advantage that I go away; for if I do not go away, the Helper will not come to you; but if I go, I will send Him to you" (John 16:7). The Lord sent us His Holy Spirit to serve as our Companion in His absence. Once we receive Jesus as Lord, others should see, hear, and observe Christ through us. We are the physical ambassadors on earth assigned and responsible for individual roles with the ultimate purpose to serve and love God as a whole.

Any woman that has received Jesus as Savior has inherently received the Holy Spirit and therefore cannot, is not, and will not ever be classified as single, alone, betrayed, or rejected again. We must be in a place to receive and pursue the love-relationship with the Holy Spirit. Whether we have been a believer and follower of Jesus for one day, one year, one decade, or one lifetime, the Holy Spirit wants a personal love-relationship with each of us. When we are pursuing love-relationships with the opposite sex, typically a relationship is first initiated because someone introduces us to that person. She was introduced to the Holy Spirit by the Teacher and his devotional teaching. She had never officially met or been formally introduced to the Holy Spirit; however, the teaching was the spark that lit her passion for responding to the love-relationship.

Have you met the Holy Spirit? God only requires us to take one step at a time. The Holy Spirit wants a personal love-relationship with you. Introduce yourself to the Holy Spirit, and He will continue to teach you more and more about Jesus and guide you into God's plan for your life. He wants to listen to you, and He wants you to listen to Him. The Holy Spirit knows everything about you and desires intimate communication in your love-relationship and to show you unconditional love. He illuminates God's Word and will anoint and equip you to complete God's plan, purpose, and calling for your life.

> "For I will restore you to health And I will heal you
> of your wounds," declares the Lord.
> —JEREMIAH 30:17

WEDNESDAY, OCTOBER 8, 2003

But the Helper, the Holy Spirit, whom the Father will send in My name, He will teach you all things, and bring to your remembrance all that I said to you.

—JOHN 14:26

A S SHE SAT in her Church mid-week, her Pastor was teaching on the ministry and calling on the Apostle Paul's life. From the pulpit he shared, "When God places a call to ministry on your life, He never takes it back." Suddenly She remembered that in June 2002, She too had answered a call to ministry.

That particular evening She had attended her friend (the Counselor's) church. The same Prophet that had prayed over her for healing had boldly proclaimed, "There's someone here with a call to ministry on your life. If that's you, I want you to come down here. I want to pray with you." The call to ministry for her was like the call to salvation. She thought her pounding heart would come out of her chest. That evening in June 2002 She had stepped out of her seat, and as the Prophet prayed in his prayer language She had prayed in her heart, *God, whatever You are asking, my answer to You is yes.* Ah, yes! She remembered that call to ministry came only days after her singleness began.

As She made her way home reflecting on her Pastor's words and the call to ministry, She had not forgotten telling God "Yes" in June 2002. She had moved forward with several ministry projects and really stepped out in faith many times over the past year. In fact, She was beginning to see Signs, Wonders, and Miracles as part of the daily norm. On the drive home, She could sense the Holy Spirit was calling her into fellowship with the Lord that evening. She could not make it home soon enough.

As She prepared for bed, She began praying and speaking to the Lord about her calling. As She wept before the Lord, She earnestly and fervently asked the Holy Spirit about her specific calling and God's plan for her ministry. *God, I know that You have called me to ministry. I do not know what you are asking me to do. Please tell me what it is!*

That is when the Lord spoke directly to her spirit, "It is a speaking Ministry. The first place you speak will be the Organization." In that moment, She believed and received the Word of the Lord. She spoke at the Organization three weeks later, and She has never turned back from her ministry calling and God's plan for her life through the Ministry.

She now remembers all that God was saying and doing on her behalf was not the end but the beginning of a love story with the Lord. Declared from the beginning, on the heels of her marriage coming to an end, and in the middle of being chronically-ill, God had a supernatural plan to orchestrate people, places, times, and resources. She had begun living her Happily Ever After.

STEP 5: CALLING

...and She has never turned back from her ministry calling and God's plan for her life through the Ministry.

As we take steps in alignment and agreement with God's instruction for our lives, His plan and purpose for our calling begins to come forth. God has a unique calling, mission, and assignment for each believer to complete for Him. Oftentimes our gifts, talents, and desires are aligned with our assignment and the Lord's greater plan and purpose for each of us.

Before She was chronically ill, She was an elementary school teacher. Educated and trained to teach students in the classroom, her heart's desire and love was teaching children. Surrendered under the guidance and influence of the Holy Spirit, She received a calling from the Lord to teach all of God's children, and the world became her classroom. God's plan for our life elevates and leads us into a direction we cannot figure out absent from worship, prayer, His Word, and obedience.

God does not rank or prioritize His calling and assignments for our lives. In our natural mindset we may assume a world famous evangelist is God's favorite and become discouraged our ministries are not as large, captivating, or popular. However, God's calling and plan is unique to us and for us.

> For there is no partiality with God.
> —ROMANS 2:11

What matters are not the opinions of others but obeying what the Holy Spirit tells us to do in service to the Lord.

One day it will be exciting to be together in heaven for eternity and see how all of our acts of obedience to the Lord produced a harvest for God's kingdom. The more we learn about God from His Word, the more apparent it becomes that "'My thoughts are not your thoughts, Nor are your ways My ways,' declares the Lord. 'For as the heavens are higher than the earth, So are My ways higher than your ways And My thoughts than your thoughts'" (Isa. 55:8–9). God's calling, plan, and purpose will always elevate us above anything we can do by ourselves.

We can always trust that when the Lord speaks through the Word, it will always come to pass. She heard from the Holy Spirit that the first place She would speak on behalf of the Ministry would be the Organization. This word was fulfilled quickly and came to pass within three weeks. Oftentimes there is time and waiting involved, and this is when and where God continues to refine and grow our faith in Him. We can be assured of our Happily Ever After but must also anticipate there is a deeper commitment in our love-relationship with the Lord.

Do you know what specific calling and ministry the Lord has for your life? God only requires us to take one step at a time. Remember that you are not responsible for figuring out God's calling on your own, but you are held accountable for obedience or disobedience to whatever plan the Lord has for your life.

> But the helper, the Holy Spirit, whom the Father will send in My name, He will teach you all things, and bring to your remembrance all that I said to you.
> —JOHN 14:26

To Be Continued...

But now faith…

—1 Corinthians 13:13

THERE IS A Happily Ever After God has planned for your life. The steps of faith shared in this part are meant to serve as guide in your love-relationship with the Lord. This is not the most important book you will ever read and is not the final authority on aligning your life and calling with God's plan for your life. The *Bible* is the first and final authority and truly is God's love letter to you personally. Prayerfully, the Lord will continue to use the testimonies of a real woman living in the real world of the twenty-first century to encourage and inspire you in your ministry calling and purpose. She has only just begun to share with you her love story. You are cordially invited to attend the wedding, because what happens next is "They Got Married."

PART II:

THEY GOT MARRIED

My heart overflows with a good theme; I address my verses to the King.

—Psalm 45:1

Sunday, November 2, 2003

Now when all the people were baptized, Jesus was also baptized, and while He was praying, heaven was opened, and the Holy Spirit descended upon Him in bodily form like a dove, and a voice came out of heaven, "You are My beloved Son, in You I am well-pleased."

—Luke 3:21–22

I DO," SHE DECLARED to the Minister as all eyes were watching and all ears were listening to her affirm her Vows. With nervous jitters and excitement over what the day symbolized, She was ecstatic to publicly declare her commitment before the Church. The changes in her life were accelerated, and for the first time the world would know of her devotion and conversion to Him. It was a day in which the past was washed away, and the public declaration of her faith in Him was being made known to friends and family. The Minister asked her if it was her testimony that Jesus was her Lord and Savior, followed by asking her to affirm that She had a call to ministry on her life. Without hesitation and with the words, "I do," She

29

was symbolically cleansed by the washing of the water before men and spiritually consecrated before her Maker.

In the months leading up to her baptism, She knew that it would be hard for those closest to her to identify with the changes in her life. As the Ministry began to take shape, She was tasked with assembling the Board, defining the Mission, and establishing the Bylaws. Progress was coming forth daily in discerning the overall reach of the Ministry. She was overjoyed to see those closest to her connecting with God's calling and plan for their lives. She continued to sense that while it was important for the Ministry to be established on a solid foundation, She must publicly establish herself with the firm foundation of Jesus.

She was searching the Scriptures daily, and there was an outpouring of opportunity for the Vision of the Ministry. Many of her friends and several family members were excited and eager to serve as Partners within the Ministry. In fact, the day She was baptized, family members as well as her friend, Courtesy, were there to support her. She and Courtesy had become trusted friends and even agreed to partner together through the Ministry. He was easy-going but seemingly supportive to go with the flow. She was learning that there was a subtle boldness required for her to step out of her past and into the destiny God had for the Ministry.

Her baptism reaffirmed her salvation publicly but was also the first time She had publicly revealed to the Church God's calling on her life. As Courtesy and the others looked on from the background, She was committing her whole self to the Ministry and tasks that lay ahead. As She arose from the water, She saw the face of Courtesy peering into the baptistery. While She could not read his thoughts, She had an uncanny sense that he was a significant part of the Ministry.

She was saying, "I do," to whatever the Lord had planned for her. The second part of her story had begun.

STEP 6: COMMITMENT

> Without hesitation and with the words, "I do," She was symbolically cleansed by the washing of the water before men and spiritually consecrated before her Maker.

Each step in the walk of faith is a progressive journey to move forward in the calling and destiny God has planned for each of our lives. There are new faces, new places, and unique personal experiences God desires for each of us. While there are similar stops on the roadmap, no two destinations into the center of God's will for our lives will be the same. Public baptism is a step of faith the Father calls each of His children to take.

For each believer the step of public baptism is an announcement to friends, family, and our church body that we have accepted Jesus as Lord and Savior of our lives. It is an external cleansing of our sins to represent the internal change within our souls, thereby, providing eternal significance. The New Testament believers modeled this baptism to publicly demonstrate personal salvation.

However, when Jesus was baptized He had no sins. As the atonement for all mankind's sins, He was not publicly cleansing Himself from sin; He was publicly consecrating Himself for the calling and destiny the Father personally had set apart for Him to accomplish. The act of Jesus' baptism was the first step before Jesus was launched into His public ministry. All the years of His life prior had been steps of preparation; however, there was a *now*-moment when Jesus had to step forward publicly to show the world

His alignment to the Father's calling, plan, and purpose for His life.

As a New Testament disciple of Christ, this same model of baptism is applicable to each of us. Prior to her baptism, She had spent time privately preparing and obeying the Lord one step at a time for the Ministry. However, her baptism represented to the Lord her commitment to surrender to the calling, plan, and purpose the Father had for both She and the Ministry. It was the launching point into the future destiny and purpose God had planned.

After Jesus was baptized, His ministry was accelerated, and so was the warfare that surrounded His calling. Once She was baptized God began supernaturally orchestrating events and opportunities. At the same time, spiritual warfare against She and the Ministry targeted both her calling and commitment. Once we publicly align ourselves with the Lord's work, subtle and overt warfare with false promises will always arise to divert our attention and ability to achieve God's plan and purposes.

Have you ever publicly identified yourself as a follower of Christ through public baptism? God only requires us to take one step at a time. While your personal ministry may be established on a solid foundation, you must publicly establish your alignment to God's plan by building your calling on the firm foundation of Jesus. Following this public step of faith, be prepared for accelerated supernatural activity manifesting itself in the natural:

> And a voice came out of heaven, "You are My beloved Son [daughter], in You I am well-pleased."
>
> —LUKE 3:22

TUESDAY, NOVEMBER 9, 2004

Thus Noah did; according to all that God had commanded him, so he did.

—GENESIS 6:22

THE MINISTRY CONTINUED to move forward. She noticed that the Lord was creating a new creation through the different Outreaches, Partnerships, and Ministry Mission. She continued to hold the Ministry in compliance with nonprofit requirements. However, she observed the Holy Spirit removing her from the ordinary experience and expectation of ministry to an extraordinary expression of the Gospel message. She knew there was a bigger platform and a more global audience than just her Board, Advisors, and Partners, so She took a step of faith and leased a Location.

For the first time the Ministry was accessible to the public, and She was placed in the position of literally building a new creation for the Lord. The inside of the Ministry did not house the typical conference and break room. The Holy Spirit was inspiring visual displays compiled of everyday objects to connect testimony and teaching opportunities through illustrative messages for Ministry Guests. The Lord brought to her remembrance the early days of elementary teaching and the high percentage of students that were visual learners. The Ministry was visually illuminating God's Word through the Dedicated Objects and testimonies within the Location.

Each day She showed up to the Location unsure and uncertain what to do next. The World had never seen anything like the Ministry, and many Critics were often cruel by scoffing, mocking, and jeering as She entered and exited the Location daily. She could identify with Noah as he built the ark. Like Noah She had to rely on specific, exact instruction and vision from God in order to move forward in her day's work. Noah's Critics were skeptical of the ark and rain, because, not unlike the Ministry, the ark and rain had never been seen. She focused each day on a renewed sense of her faith in Him in order to complete the Ministry's calling despite the Critics' responses.

As the Location continued to be transformed and re-inspired through the indwelling power of the Holy Spirit, She was able to invite many Guests to visit the Ministry. She continued to notice on an increasingly regular basis people being helped through the building of the Location. God continued to send her into Unfamiliar places throughout the region, and She met some unlikely Characters, who later became brothers and sisters in Christ. As the Lord was building a Location, He was also adding to the number daily those being saved through the Ministry (Acts 2:47).

She continued to build the Ministry Location knowing that one day the Flood of people, resources, and opportunities would present itself. As She built, She continued to speak forth all the Lord commanded her regarding the Ministry. She shared that the Ministry would one day go forth into the nations.

Look among the nations! Observe! Be astonished!
Wonder! Because *I am* doing something in your
days—You would not believe if you were told.
—HABAKKUK 1:5

She shared that each visual display was an Outreach
that connected the Word to the world. She continued to
build and speak on things that were not yet seen but only
through the lens of faith in Him.

STEP 7: CONSTRUCTION

She continued to build the Ministry Location
knowing that one day the Flood of people, resources,
and opportunities would present itself.

When the world is first introduced to a new concept or idea
within any field, there are Critics. A critical spirit is unwilling
to interrupt the daily norm or status quo ("this is how we do
it") in order to advance innovation and a spirit of creativity.
God told Noah a flood was coming and to build an ark (Gen.
6:14–7:11). Having never seen a boat or rain, Noah's call presented a double threat to the Critics in Noah's day. Noah's
responsibility was to speak the message God had given him
and move forward with the construction of the ark. This is
an example of taking steps of faith toward the calling and
plan that God had ordained for Noah and his family.

Both She and the Ministry Location received a response
similar to the one the Critics projected to Noah in his generation. Like Noah, She sought the Lord for daily instruction and relied on the Holy Spirit in order to complete each
day's work in the Location. We must realize that each day's
obedience presents the next opportunity to enter into new
seasons of growth and experience. There was a period Noah

had to gather lumber, then cut the lumber, and then fit the pieces together onto a frame of the ark. This allowed him then to seal the ark. The last step was the animals coming forth two by two. The doors were closed, and then the rain began to fall. The animals could have never come forth, had Noah not days and months and years prior been willing to gather the lumber and construct the ark. The flood would have come regardless because God said it was going to rain; however, it was Noah's responsibility to align himself with God's daily direction. There is a progression of small daily steps of obedience that are significant to fulfilling the plan and purposes of God.

Similarly, God presented to the Ministry a unique and innovative platform for the Word to be communicated. We must realize that as God builds something new in and through us, we are simultaneously being rebuilt. These steps of faith will physically, mentally, emotionally, spiritually, and financially stretch us. This part of the journey in the walk of faith with the Lord is exhausting. This is when God will deplete us of ourselves in order to refill us with Himself. God will use these seasons in our lives to continue to bring us out of our comfort zone into new environments to meet new people, be placed in new situations, and to experience new opportunities. Stepping forward with faith in Him is harder than leaving the front row pew but necessary to walk into a deeper love-relationship with the Lord.

Are you taking daily steps of faith to advance the calling God has placed on your life? God only requires us to take one step at a time. There is a Critic for every calling of God, but the Spirit's creativity and innovation supersedes the status quo of Critics' comfort zone. Continue to step forward in faith and out of your comfort zone.

> Thus Noah did; according to all that God had commanded him, so he did.
>
> —GENESIS 6:22

And I will give them one heart, and put a new spirit within them. And I will take the heart of stone out of their flesh and give them a heart of flesh.

—EZEKIEL 11:19

SHE CONTINUED TO experience God's activity and the Holy Spirit's guidance surrounding the Ministry. Each day the Lord made Himself more real and more Known to her through the study of the Word. In fact, She was amazed by how many promises were in the Bible that God had for her, her family, and the Ministry. The Lord was expanding the reach of the Ministry and her connections throughout the Nation.

Through all the changes around her and in her, She continued to develop a deeper friendship with Courtesy. She noticed a persistence and eagerness within him to join in on the Ministry activity. It had been over a year since the Ministry was birthed, and throughout its infant stages, She and Courtesy had a shared heart for the Music Outreach from the very beginning. She was amazed that

37

both the Ministry and Music Outreach were already celebrating success within its first year. With Courtesy's partnership, the Music Outreach had hosted two Concerts with nationally famous Contemporary Artists. The first Concert was a tremendous success and attendance was great. The second Concert faced more challenges than either She or Courtesy had anticipated.

She realized that the challenges were an opportunity for the Music Outreach to learn from the obstacles and continue forward in a new direction. Courtesy did not agree. For him the low Concert attendance and lack of support from Comrades at Church was enough to direct his steps away from the Music Outreach. She preserved and reaffirmed her commitment to the Ministry and continued to encourage Courtesy of his heart's desire for the Music Outreach. She reminded him that the Partnership and Music Outreach were a result of their prayers being answered and continued to seek his willingness to plan another Concert. Oddly, Courtesy's persistence and eagerness to Partner with the Ministry was replaced with resistance and avoidance following a perceived public failure with the second Concert.

She remembered her Vow to the Lord and commitment to serve, honor, and love Him. She continued to have faith in Him to accomplish what concerned her regarding Courtesy, his Comrades, and future Concerts. She continued to surrender the Music Outreach to God's Plan and purposes. She also never ceased to continue praying God's promises over Courtesy and the condition of his heart regarding the Music Outreach and partnership. The Concert experiences were the Ministry's first growing pains and a foreshadowing of challenges that would lie ahead. The Honeymoon had ended.

———— ❦ ————

STEP 8: CRITICS

> She realized that the challenges were an opportu-
> nity for the Music Outreach to learn from the obsta-
> cles and continue forward in a new direction.

Perhaps there is not a more difficult step of faith to take
than to continue moving forward when those closest to you
stop walking. In our love-relationship with the Holy Spirit,
the choice will always remain ours to walk by sight or walk
by faith. When God begins to provide us opportunity to
move forward in His assignment for our lives, the majority
of existing relationships will provide resistance. Pushback
from external circumstances will threaten the internal
commitment to the cause and platform of our calling.

It requires strength, courage, and fearless tenacity to continue moving forward in God's calling at these points in
our walk of faith. We have three decisions we can make at
this point: (1) stop walking, (2) walk backward, or (3) walk
forward. If we stop and stay where we are, refusing to move
forward, this is called partial obedience. Partial obedience
is always disobedience to the guidance of the Holy Spirit.
Giving in to the resistance and retreating back into others'
comfort zone may appease the crowd, but it will grieve the
Holy Spirit's work in our lives. Again, partial obedience is
disobedience. The consequence of our disobedience is the
hardening of our own hearts. When our hearts are hard
they no longer are sensitive to the voice and promptings
of the Holy Spirit. Without the ability to hear from or discern the voice of the Holy Spirit we cannot and will not be
equipped to complete our ministry callings or assignment
in alignment with the future God has purposed.

Courtesy decided to stay in the comfort zone and retreat
back from the calling of the Music Outreach. In contrast, She

moved forward despite the resistance from both Courtesy and his Comrades. When we are faced with this type of circumstance, we must not abandon the person in our call forward. God will bless us, our calling, and the person when we continue with intercessory prayer for the individual and circumstance (Job 42:10). Both organizations and individuals will experience (it is a guarantee) what is perceived as failure but is rather a divine opportunity to pause, pray, and reconnect to the platform and direction of the Mission.

Are you in alignment or disobedience to the calling and assignment God has ordained for your life? God only requires us to take one step at a time. You must always keep your heart sensitive and pure to discern the voice of the Holy Spirit. If you stop hearing from the Lord, your walk of faith will take you onto a strayed path from God's guidance. It is difficult to move forward against the resistance of others, but we must be willing to persevere beyond external circumstances. Although everyone may not embrace the changes Christ makes in your life, do not forsake praying for a changed heart within others. God promises in His Word:

> And I will give them one heart, and put a new spirit within them. And I will take the heart of stone out of their flesh and give them a heart of flesh.
> —EZEKIEL 11:19

Sunday, July 31, 2005

And if one can overpower him who is alone, two can resist him. A cord of three *strands* is not quickly torn apart.

—Ecclesiastes 4:12

I T WAS A milestone day that She would remember forever. As She gazed at her Child in her wedding gown, She was reminiscent of the lifetime of preparedness invested into this single moment. She was sensitive to the heart of the Father of the Bride and His willingness to give His children away into uncertain futures with trusting hands of love. She was reflective of the continued promises and months of preparedness the Lord was investing into her for a Second Marriage as well. Having a second chance at life, the Holy Spirit was teaching her what it meant to have a second chance at love.

Shortly following her answered call to the Ministry, She and her best friend, Joy, were talking on the phone, as they did most mornings. Joy lived Out of State and knew of the nitty-gritty details of her courtship with the Companion and trusted friendship with Courtesy. She and Joy were in agreement that the Lord was preparing her for a Second Marriage, yet shared a strong conviction She was not to pursue the singles approach to dating and relationships. She would remain surrendered to the calling of the Ministry and prepare herself for the man God desired as her Second Love. In addition, She would encourage other single women that God too can prepare them for a marriage without embracing the world's standard of singleness and dating.

She and Joy shared this testimony with other women on more than one occasion. Many of the women received the promise of a Second Marriage with eagerness and anticipation. Others responded with skepticism and doubt of the promise and testimony She and Joy shared. She knew that regardless of the women's responses the Lord had provided her a second chance at life and was preparing her for a Second Love.

Present-day, She was in complete agreement and continued to see the Lord's penmanship on her Child's love story. Unknown to the invited guests, as She and her Child planned the wedding they also were stepping out in faith and preparing details for the day the Lord moved on her own future husband. Her Child was both a bride and Made of Honor to stand in agreement with God's promise for her Second Marriage despite the natural circumstances. She continued to have faith in Him that God was in every detail of her life and continued to pursue her love-relationship with Him. She realized that once God spoke over her and her Second Marriage, nothing on earth held the power to separate the Union, "What therefore God has joined together, let no man separate" (Matt. 19:6).

STEP 9: CEREMONY

> She was sensitive to the heart of the Father of the Bride and His willingness to give His children away into uncertain futures with trusting hands of love.

God is our Father who neither slumbers nor sleeps (Ps. 121:4). He is always active and never accomplishing only one task at a time. He holds times and seasons in His hand, and as we continue in our walk with the Lord we will begin to discern His activity. When we truly surrender ourselves and agenda to the Lord, our actions, decisions, and thoughts will become integrated into the plan and purposes of God.

As She continued forward in the professional calling of the Ministry, the Lord began guiding and directing the steps of her personal life. She and Joy were in agreement and stood in faith believing that one day She would have a Second Marriage. She realized that the same guidance from the Word and Biblical obedience to God's standard of preparation not only applied to the Ministry but also to her personal preparedness for her Second Love. Similarly, we must allow the Holy Spirit to work in every area of our life in order to lead a transformed life. As this surrender occurs, our walk with the Lord will no longer be compartmentalized as professional or personal decisions. Rather, we will become vessels that are joined together, much like a bride and groom, becoming one with the Father's will and purposes.

As She stood in faith believing in God's promise to prepare her for a Second Marriage, She moved forward and activated her faith in Him. The season of preparing for her Child's wedding allowed her to take steps in preparing details for her own. We must align ourselves with those who will stand in agreement for God's work to be completed through our lives. Unbelief is the opposite of faith and the absolute enemy to our faith walk with the Lord. If the enemy can cause us to enter into unbelief, he can steal our testimony and ultimately the assignment God has for our lives.

As She continued to prepare for her Second Marriage, God was accomplishing more than one task through this promise. The Holy Spirit was also sharing the testimony to encourage other single women in their love-relationship with both the Lord and men. Both her personal and professional lives were being integrated into God's calling. The surrendered life becomes an integrated life to demonstrate God's sovereignty through our love-relationship with the Lord.

Are you allowing God to transform every area of your life? God only requires us to take one step at time. You can be confident that God holds the times and seasons in His hand and also requires us to align our thoughts and actions in agreement with His Word. Once God speaks, His Word will be manifested in the natural. You must stand in agreement with God as a believing remnant and not enter into unbelief based on God's appointed times for His promises.

> And if one can overpower him who is alone, two can resist him. A cord of three *strands* is not quickly torn apart.
>
> —ECCLESIASTES 4:12

SATURDAY, APRIL 7, 2007

The nations will see your righteousness, And all kings your glory; and you will be called by a new name Which the mouth of the Lord will designate.

—ISAIAH 62:2

AS SHE CONTINUED to live by faith, it was becoming more and more challenging financially. She had obeyed God by leasing the Location. She had continued to maintain the family estate for her Children. She was learning what it was like being a Single woman with a Ministry in today's world. She continued to press into the Word daily and learned more and more about God's economic system and view of money from the Wise Man of the East. She was practicing the Biblical principles of sowing tithes and offerings into her Church, as well as, other ministries. Yet in spite of her obedience, financial pressures arose.

The Wise Man shared that when extreme financial pressure arises, rather than focusing on the problem, focus on giving. The Wise Man shared testimony of his Operation facing threats of closure and failure in the early days. She learned about the Law of Reciprocity and how what we receive is in direct connection to what we give. By not only demonstrating her faith in Him to believe but also activating her faith through specific acts of obedience, She began to witness a gradual change in her finances.

> Give, and it will be given to you…
> —LUKE 6:38

One day her cell phone rang, and it was a local Guardian on the phone. The Guardian shared that many famous Hollywood Celebrities were in town to film a movie and were in need of homes to lease while visiting. One of the movie stars was interested in living in her family estate home while in town for two months. The Guardian shared that not only was financial provision attached, but She could also personally service the cleaning of the home, with additional provision being provided. The Lord sent in His Portion, which was enough to meet the Ministry's financial responsibilities and provide for her as well for the remainder of the year. She realized that not only was God providing for His Ministry, but He was also sending in the "hidden wealth of secret places" in the process (Isa. 45:3). While living her daily life in obedience and surrender, the Lord was demonstrating His power to provide for both She and the Ministry in ways that superseded human reasoning and logic.

She had known the Lord as Healer and was learning His ways as Provider and His desire to daily provide His Portion for her. He too was showing and sharing with her how much she was loved by Him. The Lord's sovereignty was guiding and directing her life into a future of excitement, and She was trusting Him with a deeper level of surrender and commitment. It was a love-relationship dreamed by romantics but a reality found through the pages of the Word. It was not always glamorous, popular, or easy keeping her Vow; but the Lord was Beloved by her and She was Darling to Him.

STEP 10: CURRENCY

> She continued to press into the Word daily and learned more and more about God's economic system and view of money...

Our God is sovereign. He is all-knowing over all circumstances all the time. While we have a free will, His desire is for us to recognize the voice and promptings of the Holy Spirit in order to be change agents for His kingdom throughout the earth. Financial pressure and hardships are perhaps the most dominant strategy of the enemy to divert God's children away from the Lord's guidance. Authentic discipleship is not giving in or giving up in the face of trying times or external pressures. When financial pressure is an external threat to your calling and destiny, it is time to internally draw strength and power from God's economy.

In the Old Testament when men or women overcame a significant hardship or battle either the person or place would receive a new name. The journey to victory was years in the making and marked with experience after experience of suffering, pressure, and the false impression that enemies were triumphing over God's people. In reality, each experience was an opportunity to learn more about God's character and intervention on behalf of His children. This Old Testament heritage was a foreshadowing of Christ's victory and assigning a new name to each of His children in triumph over every area of suffering.

Likewise, through each step in our faith walk with

the Lord, we learn more names that God personally reveals Himself to be: Savior, Healer, Teacher, Comforter, Companion, Redeemer, Friend, and Beloved. She had come to know the Lord as all of these names; however, She came to know Him as Provider through the financial season of lack. Likewise, throughout the journey the Lord let her be known to Him by a new name. She was Darling, and He was her Beloved. Through the unity, agreement, commitment to the Vow, and faith in Him, She was in love.

Are you experiencing suffering or financial hardship? God only requires us to take one step at a time. The Lord wants you know Him as Provider. It is always the darkest before the dawn breaks through into Light. God will set the stage where He is the only One who can get the honor, glory, or praise for your miracle. In the process, you will learn the Character of God and come to know Him by a new name. Likewise, "You will be called by a new name Which the mouth of the Lord will designate" (Isa. 62:2).

To Be Continued...

But now faith, hope...

—1 Corinthians 13:13

WEDDINGS ARE A joyous occasion where a man and woman share with the world their vow to honor and love each other, solely and exclusively. The intimacy and unity shared is deeply personal and sacred between the couple. Likewise, God's desire is for a love-relationship with you that is intricately woven into every area of your life. The Holy Spirit longs to be a part of the daily details of your life, and the Father is honored each time you remember your vows to the Lord. The steps of faith shared in this book are meant to serve as a guide in your love-relationship with the Lord.

This is not the most important book you will ever read and is not the final authority on aligning your life and calling with God's plan for your life. The *Bible* is the first and final authority and truly is God's love letter to you personally. Prayerfully, the Lord will continue to use the testimonies of a real woman living in the real world of the twenty-first century to encourage and inspire you in your ministry, calling and purpose.

Just like a marriage is filled with ups and downs, so is the discovery of love that is experienced as time continues in a marriage relationship. She has only just begun to share with you her love story. Next, they "Fell in Love."

PART III:

THEY FELL IN LOVE

And in Your book were all written the days that were ordained *for me*, When as yet there was not one of them.

—PSALM 139:16

Tuesday, September 1, 2009

Now the Lord said to Abram, "Go forth from your country, And from your relatives And from your father's house, To the land which I will show you; And I will make you a great nation, And I will bless you, And make your name great; And so you shall be a blessing; And I will bless those who bless you, And the one who curses you I will curse."

—Genesis 12:1–3

I T WAS SEEMINGLY the end of the new Life God had created. Like Noah, She had spent years of faithful service to God building and creating a new work for the Lord. Now, suddenly the Ministry was being called forth into Storage. As the Ministry had continued to move forward She was faced with new challenges and trusted God to intervene on her behalf through each situation. However, this time it was different. She did not know where the Ministry would be located, how She was to complete her calling, nor what God was requiring of her. The Lord had been teaching her to identify with the circumstances

His children experienced in the Word. She sensed that like Abraham, God was calling both She and the Ministry into an Unknown destiny and future.

So like Abraham, after praying, fasting, and seeking God, She resolutely obeyed the Lord. As She dissembled the dozens of teaching displays representative of almost five years of work, She cried tears of Fatigue. As She moved the Dedicated Objects into a dusty, dark, and far-removed space, She cried tears of Frustration. She cried aloud with faith in Him that God's Plan was better than her best-made plans. Despite the tears, She found herself and the Ministry in a new place, surrounded by the Unfamiliar. At that moment, She realized that if God did not intervene on behalf of the Ministry, there would be no Ministry. The work was not of her strength or power but was a result of the Holy Spirit speaking the Father's will and direction.

With the Ministry in Storage, She did the only thing She could do at this point. She sought the Lord. The Critics all shared their opinions over what God was doing. Many thought She should return to the elementary class-room to teach, affirming She certainly was good at that job and enticing her that the reliable salary was a perk. Others criticized that She had misused the resources God had provided her time and time again. Yet, as She pursued God's plan through the Word, the instruction She was receiving said none of these things. She would listen to the Lord.

The Lord began to show her that Abraham had a moment of ultimate sacrifice in which God intervened to turn around his circumstance. She realized that God was calling her away from the land that was called home in order to release the Promised Land into the life of the Ministry and her Family. She had faithfully followed the Lord into the Wilderness, and He was showing her not only how to survive and thrive in this place but how to successfully journey through to the other side. God had a Plan of Redemption.

STEP 11: CHANGE

> She realized that God was calling her away from the land that was called home in order to release the Promised Land into the life of the Ministry and her Family.

In the faith-walk with the Lord, a repeat Culprit to the destiny and future God has for each of us is the Unknown. The unsettling, unnerving, unexpected, and unfamiliar qualities of the Unknown make the settled, comfortable, and expected lifestyle of the Known appear as the place where God is working and moving. However, we must remember that God is the only unchanging part of our lives.

> Jesus Christ is the same yesterday and today and forever.
>
> —HEBREWS 13:8

Circumstances will always change around us, which is why we must always know the direction God is adjusting our lives and moving us toward. When we stay in step with Him, the Father is already there waiting for us. He planned our future; He knows our created destiny. In order to defeat the Unknown, the voice of the Holy Spirit can always be trusted and should always supersede any aspect of the familiar.

God's Word provides the model for aligning our lives to God's plan and purposes. We have unique access to glean insight and truth from the experiences shared in Scripture.

She realized that like Abraham, God was calling her into an Unknown future, but that through complete obedience and sacrifice the blessings far outweighed the hesitations. In addition to the Unknown being a repeat Culprit in the faith-walk with the Lord, Critics are repeat characters to prevent us from moving forward in our love-relationship.

> Do you still want to argue with the Almighty? You are God's critic, but do you have the answers?
> —Job 40:2, NLT

In her season of transition, God was the only One She could turn to in order to guide both She and the Ministry through the Wilderness. The Father's plan will never conform to peoples' agenda or opinions, but He will transform people according to His plan. When facing Critics, never stop praying for them, but do not adjust His purposes according to their platform.

Are you moving toward or away from the Promised Land God has waiting? God only requires us to take one step at a time. When God begins to move you toward the Promised Land, it will be tempting to fall back on the gifts, talents, and resources God has used to prepare you for your calling. You must recognize the preparation is a catalyst to propel you forward, not a safety net to fall back on in difficult seasons. God's promises always come to pass, and His plan and instruction is found in the Word. The circumstances God places you in define the outcome of your future. From the beginning, God has always had a Plan of Redemption. Jesus was and is and will forever be the Plan of Redemption. We must listen and follow Him "to the land which I will show you" (Gen. 12:1).

Friday, February 4, 2010

Then the Lord said to Moses, "Why are you crying out to Me? Tell the sons of Israel to go forward."

—Exodus 14:15

As the Ministry remained in Storage She remained in the Word. Ironically, the Ministry and Lord's work continued to move forward despite the physical Location of the building. She was experiencing a new level of reliance on God in the Wilderness. This was not a season She wanted to stay in for forty years, like the wandering Israelites (Deut. 29:5). She continued to notice that as each act of obedience presented itself, God was accelerating His activity in her life. Likewise, there was a daily reliance on the provision and sustenance of the Lord to guide her. In the Wilderness, there was not a professional Ministry guide to serve as the blueprint for survival. Rather, the instruction for both She and the Ministry was being released through her daily study with the Lord. God's Word was the map leading the Ministry through this season.

Through the Wilderness experience, She continued to seek the Lord's guidance for financial provision, and She always received just enough Daily Bread to sustain both She and the Ministry. The season of Lack had ended, and the season of Just Enough presented a new series of opportunities to demonstrate reliance on the Lord as Provider. She relied on the Lord to direct her spending, her time, and her decisions in agreement and alignment to the Father's plan. The Holy Spirit began to speak bold revelations to her regarding the family estate home, her Children, and the Ministry. She knew His voice and the importance of complete obedience to the Lord. So after fasting, praying, and studying the Word, She received and believed God's instruction to lead both She and the Ministry into the Promised Land.

Part of the Plan included the Lord's instruction to release the family estate home to her Children as an early inheritance. It was the most valuable possession She personally owned, and after receiving Wise Counsel, She knew the Lord was revealing a deeper level of being her Provider. He was now her Husband, and He was faithfully devoted to her. She knew that by releasing the home to her Children, She and the Ministry would be provided for, although the future was uncertain since the Ministry was housed in the Wilderness. She questioned her obedience when only one Child accepted the free gift, while the other declined the inheritance. While She could relate to the pain of the Father's heart when His children do not accept the gifts, inheritance, and abundance He freely offers, She also believed in His promises and His ability to continually guide both Children into the center of His unique and personal Plan for each of their futures. In the final moments of February 4, 2010, the time came, and She knew it was the moment of moving forward with the Plan.

She called her Child and declared it was time to go forward. She too prepared for action and aligned herself by faith in Him to God's Plan. At that time, neither She nor her family knew what they were moving toward. Yet, in that moment there was a shift of seeing God's sovereignty, protection, and provision manifest over the Ministry calling and the Characters involved. She had declared her citizenship in Miracle Territory, and in the days to come She and the Ministry became residents of the Promised Land. Yet, to her surprise there were Giants waiting for her when She arrived.

STEP 12: CULPRITS

> She had declared her citizenship in Miracle Territory, and in the days to come She and the Ministry became residents of the Promised Land.

Of all the steps in the journey of our faith-walk, perhaps the most defining moment is when God reveals it is time to enter the Promised Land. This step represents past successes and assures future challenges that exceed self-sufficiency for survival in the new Land. In other words, we cannot reside in the Land of Promise for our calling on our own strength. The series of experiences leading up to the monumental shift in the natural and supernatural are past victories for the Lord's work in and through us; however, there is a deeper level of total reliance (spiritual, physical, emotional, and financial) on God once we arrive in the Promised Land.

The Promised Land is foreign. Just as there would be times of acclamation while traveling to any place for the first time, the Promised Land represents a similar experience in our faith-walk. There will be new people, new opportunities, new levels of blessings, new challenges, and greater victories. While we may be entering a new culture, it is also important to remember that in essence we are likewise becoming citizens of a new realm, Miracle Territory.

The Israelites had seen God intervene on their behalf in Egypt; they knew without a doubt that God loved them and would save and deliver them from bondage. In the Wilderness, God's people could also identify that He provides for His children and will refine their character and define their calling in this season. Yet, the Promised Land is what God desires to release in order to bless us and, more importantly, position us to bless others.

This part of the faith-walk is deeply personal and unique to our love-relationship with the Lord. She spent six months in the Wilderness season; the Israelites spent forty years. There is no formula for this part of the journey, but rather God will present a series of extreme circumstances to strengthen our reliance on Him. We can be certain that each day God will provide enough manna for that day. The Wilderness is a holding place. The Promised Land is a Holy Place. The Lord prepares us in the Wilderness to be a Temple transformed from a holding place of His power to a Holy Place of His complete presence.

> Do you not know that you are a temple of God and
> *that* the Spirit of God dwells in you?
> —1 CORINTHIANS 3:16

Are you ready to become a resident of Miracle Territory in your faith-walk with the Lord? God only requires us to take one step at a time. There are no shortcuts into the Promised Land; you must cross through the Wilderness. The biggest miracle is always connected to giving when you are in the position of having the least. God will provide for you in the Wilderness, and you will survive. Yet to thrive with the gifts, talents, and calling He has given you requires a pursuit and declaration to stop crying and "go forward" (Exod. 14:15).

Friday, October 15, 2010

And He said to them, "Follow Me, and I will make you fishers of men."

—Matthew 4:19

L IVING IN MIRACLE Territory, She began to see Signs, Wonders, and Miracles as part of the daily norm. God was in the details. His love for both her and the Ministry was revealing itself in the everyday decisions in her faith-walk with the Lord. Shortly after She released the family estate to her Child as an inheritance, She moved into the Land of Promise. It was then God opened a new door for the Ministry Headquarters to be housed in a larger Temple. Although grateful for the new site, She noticed that the Ministry's work was accomplished wherever God sent her rather than being limited to four walls. Yet, despite the continued favor in the Promised Land, nothing prepared her for the next part of God's Plan.

In May of 2010, She received a call that her Prodigal Brother had returned home. After a crashed course in life, he was living in the Country that neighbored her new location in the Promised Land. She spent many hours traveling back and forth to her Prodigal Brother's Country as well as, in deep intercession for God's guidance for his future. One day She received a call that eighteen acres of land was for sale. The land housed a cabin, a home, and two ponds. Many of the Onlookers shared this would be a great spot for the Prodigal Brother to resettle his unsettled life.

She prayed, and She shared her concerns with the Lord and the Ministry Partners (who at this time were scattered across the Nation). While God was providing Just Enough for her needs, neither She nor the Ministry were in a position to purchase the land for the Prodigal Brother. However, while God was providing her Just Enough, He was providing one of the Partners with More than Enough. To her surprise, She received a Donation from one of these Partners to purchase the land for the Ministry.

As She signed the papers for the eighteen acres on behalf of the Ministry, a newfound sense of awe in the Lord was experienced. She spoke with her Prodigal Brother about living on the land and maintaining the grounds. He shared he preferred to remain in the Country he was currently residing. The Holy Spirit revealed to her that the land was to be called "Fishers of Men Retreat" and would host gatherings, retreats, and guests on the grounds. He also brought to her remembrance that "Fishers of Men" was a teaching display housed in the Ministry's Old Location. The Lord showed her that the prophetic testimonies were now going forth from the Old Location into the earth.

As She rejoiced in the Signs, Wonders, and Miracles of the Lord and His work, She noticed that those in the new Country did not. She was sensitive to the new region and its strongholds, which were different than her own region. Despite the challenges, the Lord had equipped her with a different spirit to defeat these Giants in Jesus' name. Throughout the journey, the Ministry would disciple others through their faith-walk to become Fishers of Men.

STEP 13: CULTURE

> Although grateful for the new site, She noticed that the Ministry's work was accomplished wherever God sent her rather than being limited to four walls.

God's Plan is always found in the details. He is never only penning one love story; rather, the lives of others become interwoven and intersected through our love-relationship with the Lord. Moments that at the time may seem insignificant in hindsight will reflect God's sovereignty and intervention in the circumstance. In the Promised Land, the faith-walk with the Lord is transferred to meeting the needs of those around us. In the process, God's provision and purposes are glorified magnificently.

After She released what She was holding on to, a family estate, God released what He was holding; a Ministry Headquarters and eighteen acres of Land.[1] In addition, the day She received the call her Prodigal Brother had returned

---

1 In less than a year after releasing the family estate, the Ministry received a donation to purchase eighteen acres of land in October 2010. In January 2011, the Ministry received an adjoining tract of twelve acres with an additional pond, barn, and home. Praise God!

home was a testament to answered prayer. However, at the time She could not anticipate that in the process of rebuilding a man the Lord would also be building and expanding the Ministry.

In the Promised Land, God will always broaden our territory and stretch us beyond our capacity. This process is ongoing and on purpose. If we rely on our personal strength and abilities in the Promised Land, we will stifle the Signs and Wonders of Miracle Territory. As a result, our Promised Land will simply become a new place of captivity (Egypt) later marked by a new Wilderness experience. In the Promised Land there are cultural variations. We must be globally sensitive to the differences in values, norms, and lifestyles when entering new regions. Although the Prodigal Brother's Country was located in regional proximity, it was a foreign experience for the Ministry. She invested time traveling to and fro the new Country in order to experience the culture.

In the Promised Land, we must always understand that there are preexisting Giants residing in the territory. The Giants will reveal themselves only when they perceive the work being done is a threat to their Land. As the Ministry began restoring and preparing the land for the Retreat, She saw the strongholds and opposition manifest themselves. When Moses assigned the twelve spies to assess the Promised Land, only two came back with a favorable report (Num. 13:25–33). The other ten, along with their families, perished in the Wilderness. Joshua and Caleb were allowed by God to enter the Promised Land because they had a different spirit. To remain victorious in the Promised Land of our calling, we must always look to the Lord and never at the size of the Giants.

Are you looking at God or the Giants in the Promised Land? God only requires us to take one step at time. It takes a different spirit, the Holy Spirit, to navigate and direct the

Promised Land phase of the journey. Whatever the culture or calling of your Promised Land, Jesus' invitation and promise is simply, "Follow Me, and I will make you fishers of men" (Matt. 4:19).

SATURDAY, OCTOBER 8, 2011

Now faith is the assurance of *things* hoped for, the conviction of things not seen.

—HEBREWS 11:1

SHE GATHERED WITH the Partners to celebrate the eight-year anniversary of the Ministry being called forth by the Lord. It had been eight years since the Lord revealed to her the plans and calling for the Ministry, and She was amazed at the journey He had taken her on in that time span. She had stepped out with faith in Him to publicly declare her calling, to lease the Old Location, to prophetically announce God was preparing her for a Second Marriage, to rise above the Critics, to move from the Wilderness to the Promised Land, to rely on the Lord for provision, to release her only possession as an inheritance, to cross into a new Country, and to prepare acreage for Ministry outreaches and opportunities.

She had learned from the Wise Man of the East that in Scripture the number eight signifies a New Beginning. She was entering the season of a New Beginning for the Ministry, and She could not contain the expectation or anticipation of the Lord's activity and direction to refine and redefine this New Beginning. She praised God with the Partners for the dozens of Outreaches that had been declared through the Ministry; over half were active and producing fruit in the earth. She worshiped the Lord for being her Savior, Healer, Deliverer, Companion, Counselor, Provider, Teacher, and Husband. She repented to the Father over her shortcomings along the journey and for any time her mistakes on the Ministry confused the ultimate will and work of the Lord. She announced that in the days, weeks, months, and years to come the Signs, Wonders, and Miracles to and from the Ministry would represent a New Beginning.

She reflected over the promises made by the Lord to both She and the Ministry. She pondered what would occur with the Partners that fell away from their Ministry calling. She treasured the remnant that pursued their calling despite the pressure from Critics or Giants. She interceded that in the New Beginning hearts of stone would be transformed into hearts of flesh. She thanked God that He had sustained not only the Ministry but also her family through the journey of beginning and building the Ministry. Her First Love had remarried and was living his New Beginning. Her Child's inheritance had not only survived a divorce but was thriving in the Land of Promise. She welcomed the presence of the Lord to usher in the glory and transforming power of God over the New Beginning in every detail of her life.

There was no doubt God had blessed both She and the Ministry with favor and grace over the past eight years. She was so grateful and thankful of the fulfillment of God's Word for her life. She thanked God for His many gifts to her and perhaps was most grateful for the gift of faith in Him. The Lord had bestowed on her the gift of faith. Every promise and every Word God spoke forth over her life, She believed. She did not have faith in the natural circumstances, but rather her faith was grounded in the Character of God. The Ministry could celebrate the monumental milestones because God had extended to her faith in Him. She believed God's promises and stood firm in the conviction that every declaration of the Lord would come to pass. It was a New Beginning, and She stood firm in the remembrance that the end had been declared from the beginning.

STEP 14: CELEBRATION

> She was entering the season of a New Beginning for the Ministry, and She could not contain the expectation or anticipation of the Lord's activity and direction to refine and redefine this New Beginning.

God is long-suffering; He is eternal. Every plan, every purpose, and every act of obedience He calls us to is an opportunity to ultimately partner with God in His Plan. There is only One God in the universe; He is the Alpha and Omega, the Beginning and the End (Rev. 22:13). He created man in His own image (Gen. 1:26). There is only One God, and there is only one of each of us designed to fulfill His Plan. The faith-walk with the Lord is not about the destination. As believers we know where we will ultimately spend eternity—heaven. The faith-walk with the Lord is about the journey. It is centered on willingness and obedience to align our actions, thoughts, and words to God's Plan. The faith-walk with the Lord is not a giant leap from earth into our eternal destination. It is a daily step-by-step process to be transformed into the likeness of Christ through the empowering and equipping of the Holy Spirit.

The more we fall in love with the Lord the more we realize the depths of love found in His character. The more time we spend praising God through our worship; interceding through prayer; studying the Word; and giving of our time, talents, and resources, we will daily experience a transformation that touches not only our lives but the lives of our family, friends, and coworkers. We will not have to seek out opportunities to share the gospel. Our lives will become a living example of the gospel and God's Plan of Redemption. Our callings and God's signature of sovereignty will become evidence bearing His Plan in every layer of society.

Oftentimes couples who have been married for decades will share that their love for their spouse has deepened over time, more so than the love shared on their wedding day. The same is true for the Lord. In the early days of the love-relationship with the Lord there is an infatuation with the Happily Ever After. However, once They Got Married the commitment grows into a more meaningful love as time provides experiences and opportunities together. One day, a couple will look up and celebrate commemorated anniversaries to highlight the journey thus far and anticipate the continuation of their love story. This is why the eight-year New Beginning was such a milestone for both her and the Ministry. It was a time to celebrate the past journey and prepare for the future destination, on earth and for eternity.

Can you identify God's sovereign hand guiding your calling? God only requires us to take one step at a time. To see God's promises come to pass in your life, you must simply believe what God says and align your actions, thoughts, and words with His Word. There are specific times of preparation and growth, as well as, milestone markers to celebrate the journey. As you continue to move forward in the love-relationship with the Lord, faith in Him is the cornerstone of advancing His agenda daily.

> Now faith is the assurance of *things* hoped for, the conviction of things not seen.
>
> —HEBREWS 11:1

SUNDAY, JANUARY 1, 2012

Declaring the end from the beginning, And from ancient times things which have not been done, Saying, "My purpose will be established, And I will accomplish all My good pleasure;" Calling a bird of prey from the east, The man of My purpose from a far country. Truly, I have spoken; truly I will bring it to pass. I have planned *it, surely* I will do it.

—ISAIAH 46:10–11

SHE AWOKE AMAZED by the year gone by and with anticipation of the New Year. In the final hours of 2011, the Lord had broken off the last idol of Egypt from her life. She had released her luxury vehicle to her Child and had purchased a new Chariot. It was a lifetime purchase She had never experienced. She was learning more and more that the Lord was a generous Husband. She was truly free from the lifetime of servitude to materialism and any tangible possession connected to Egypt. The Lord was making every detail of her life a fresh start in the New Beginning.

She was months away from experiencing a life of

Restoration in the New Year. Part of the Plan in the Promised Land was abundance, increase, and excess. Yet, She knew that the Promised Land was not attributed to her strength but rather the Lord's manifestations that were being poured forth over both She and the Ministry. She was not reliant on a natural man but keenly aware that the new standard of living demonstrated the Lord's desire for His Bride.

In the days ahead, She and her family were cruising to the Islands. When She awoke in the New Year, She knew God had opened the door of faith. However, She did not anticipate the Miracle Territory awaiting the Ministry when She arrived. Also, in the months ahead the Ministry would host a Tent Revival at the Land. She knew that God had promised souls to enter His kingdom. She could not plan for or predict the magnitude of the outpouring of His Spirit in the process. In the year ahead, She would continue to receive God's Promise to her for a future husband. She could not fathom the depths of the Lord's vision for the fulfillment of this Promise. She knew that it was coming to pass without delay, as the Father of the Bride continued to speak to her about the Second Love that was worthy of her heart and hand.

She had faith in Him that the Ministry was the Lord's and that She was His Love. The Plan was better than her own imagination. The Vision was bigger than her personal desires and dreams. She had faith in Him that She had only just begun learning to live in the Promised Land. It was a daily process of surrender to experience the culture and community within Miracle Territory. She was living her Happily Ever After, which had been declared from the beginning. After They Got Married, She remained steadfast in her Vow to the Lord. And, every day a New Chapter of They Fell in Love was being written. It was a Story written not by human hands but inspired by the fingertips of God. In the end She had faith in Him, and that was really the beginning of her Love Story.

STEP 15: COVENANT

> She knew that it was coming to pass without delay, as the Father of the Bride continued to speak to her about the Second Love that was worthy of her heart and hand.

In the love-relationship with the Lord, we are the Bride of Christ. God is the Father of the Bride, the Holy Spirit is the Best Man, and Jesus is the Bridegroom. The Lord is coming back for His Bride and will not leave us, fail us, or forsake us with broken vows or unfulfilled promises (Heb. 3:7). As each of our love stories is being written through the pursuit of our created destiny and calling, God is preparing His children for a life of Promise on earth and for eternity.

Faith steps that appear small or insignificant may actually be monumental leaps in preparing for the future God wants to release into our lives. For example, as a bride prepares for her wedding day there are significant days of joy, such as selecting the perfect dress or wedding cake. These are glamorous, exciting, once-in-a-lifetime joys. However, other days of preparation may not be as exciting but rather tedious, stressful, and quite the chore. While preparing for the wedding the bride must also dedicate time to collecting names and addresses for the guest list. All of these actions are important to the wedding day being a success, although some are more enjoyable than others. If the bride dismissed the guest list it would be a great disappointment on the wedding day when there were no friends or family in attendance. The bride must see the end from the beginning in each step of preparation.

The same is true in our faith-walk with the Lord. We know the end from the beginning. Jesus is returning for His Bride. As believers we have assurance of salvation in heaven. But, how disappointed we will be to show up and discover that days on earth we dismissed as cumbersome were in reality extremely important to the Big Day. As believers we are invited to the Marriage Supper of the Lamb (Rev. 19:9). We will sit with the Lord as His Bride, and each of us will be awarded for our obedience to the Father. The love-relationship with the Lord is a day-by-day, trusted willingness to prepare for eternity. As we are aligning our lives in obedience to the Father, we are aiding in helping others be prepared for the Marriage Supper as well.

Are you prepared for the Big Day of seeing the Bridegroom? God only requires us to take one step at time. God is sovereign, and we can trust each act of obedience has a specific purpose attached to fulfill the plan He has in mind for our lives. Continue to allow God to write your love story as He speaks forth His plan for your life through the Holy Spirit. You can confidently know the end from the beginning; however, the willingness to take the journey is the great joy of being friends in Him.

> Truly, I have spoken; truly I will bring it to pass. I have planned *it, surely* I will do it.
>
> —Isaiah 46:11

To Be Continued . . .

But now faith, hope, love, abide these three; but the greatest of these is love.

—1 Corinthians 13:13

THE FAITH-WALK WITH the Lord involves surrender to trust and align our lives in agreement to the Plan of the Father. As you journeyed through the pages of this book, prayerfully you discovered that each step was guided through the Word.

This parable series is not the most important book you will ever read and is not the final authority on aligning your life and calling with God's plan for your life. The *Bible* is the first and final authority and truly is God's love letter to you personally. Prayerfully, the Lord will continue to use the testimonies of a real woman, living in the real world of the twenty-first century to encourage and inspire you in your ministry, calling, and purpose.

The *Bible* is the Love Story written for you personally to learn from and live by as God authors your story. While the end of God's Plan of Redemption has been written from the beginning (see Genesis 3), you are the only character He created to fulfill the role of the leading lady in your story.

The testimonies shared are not just the story of Redemption for She, her family, and the Ministry; they are a testament to the story of Redemption God has authored for you. Present-day, She and the Ministry continue to move forward in their faith-walk. The journey of meeting new characters in new places is a day-by-day experience She will celebrate in preparation for the Big Day. She looks forward to you attending the Marriage Supper of the Lamb. God only requires us to take one step at a time.

> The Lord of hosts has sworn saying, "Surely, just as I have intended so it has happened, and just as I have planned so it will stand... For the Lord of hosts has planned, and who can frustrate *it*? And as for His stretched-out hand, who can turn it back?"
> —ISAIAH 14:24, 27

To Be Continued . . .

Stay tuned for the second story of
Friends in Him: Our Walk of Faith

It's Coming Soon!

Special thanks to our friends in Him at
Creation House Publishing for walking out
this journey with us.

Contact the Author

Friends in Him are invited to contact and connect with Dr. Brooke Mitchell at www.ThroneRoomConsulting.com

...And you will be called, "Sought out"...

—Isaiah 62:12

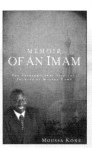